10

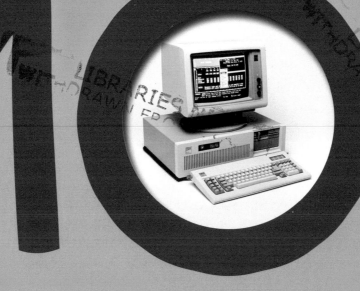

IDEAS
THAT CHANGED
THE WORLD

Written by Cath Senker

WAYLAND
www.waylandbooks.co.uk

First published in 2015 by Wayland
Copyright © Wayland, 2015

Editors: Julia Adams; Katie Woolley
Designer: Peter Clayman

Dewey number: 303.4'83–dc23
ISBN 978 0 7502 9139 2
Library eBook ISBN 978 0 7502 9140 8

Printed in China

10 9 8 7 6 5 4 3 2 1

Picture acknowledgements: Cover: © Martin Moxter/imageBROKER/Corbis; back cover (top left): © Stefano Bianchetti/Corbis; back cover (bottom right): © Corbis; p. 1, p. 3 (bottom, 5th from left), p. 25: © Bettmann/Corbis; p. 2 (bottom, far left), p. 7: © George Tiedemann/GT images/Corbis; p. 2 (bottom, 2nd from left), p. 9: © Simon Balson/Alamy; p. 2 (bottom, 3rd from left), p. 11: © Corbis; p. 2 (bottom, 4th from left), p. 4 (top), p. 13: © Corbis; p. 2 (bottom, 5th from left), p. 15: © Hulton-Deutsch Collection/Corbis; p.3 (bottom, far left), p. 17: © Ann Johansson/Corbis; p. 3 (bottom, 2nd from left), p. 19: © Stefano Bianchetti/Corbis; p. 3 (3rd from left), p. 21: © Schenectady Museum; Hall of Electrical History Foundation/Corbis; p. 4 (bottom), p. 20: © Gianni Dagli Orti/Corbis; p. 6 (top): © BeBa/iberfoto/Mary Evans; p. 6 (bottom): © Corbis; p. 8: © Araldo de Luca/Corbis; p. 10: © Mary Evans Picture Library; p. 12: © Sten Schunke/Westend61/Corbis; p. 14, p. 30: © Michael Nicholson/Corbis; p. 16: © Corbis; p. 18: © Underwood & Underwood/Corbis; p. 22, p. 31: © Corbis; p. 24: © Bettmann/Corbis; p. 26 (top right): © Gianni Dagli Orti/Corbis; p. 26 (top centre): © Bettmann/Corbis; p. 26 (centre): © Chris Cheadle/All Canada Photos/Corbis; p. 26 (bottom): © Tetra images/Corbis; p. 27 (top right): © Hulton-Deutsch Collection/Corbis; p. 27 (centre left): © Schenectady Museum; Hall of Electrical History; p. 27 (centre right): © Minnesota Historical Society/Corbis; p. 28 (top): © Stapleton Collection/Corbis; p. 28 (centre): © GraphicaArtis/Corbis; p. 29 (top): © Stapleton Collection/Corbis; p. 32: © Tom Grill/Corbis; all images used as graphic elements: Shutterstock.

The website addresses (URLs) included in this book were valid at the time of going to press. However, it is possible that contents or addresses may change following the publication of this book. No responsibility for any such changes can be accepted by either the author or the Publisher.

Every attempt has been made to clear copyright. Should there be any inadvertent omission, please apply to the publisher for rectification.

Wayland, an imprint of Hachette Children's Group
Part of Hodder & Stoughton
Carmelite House
50 Victoria Embankment
London
EC4Y 0DZ

An Hachette UK Company
www.hachette.co.uk
www.hachettechildrens.co.uk

MIX
Paper from responsible sources
FSC® C104740

Contents

INTRODUCTION

In this book are ten significant ideas that changed the world, ranging throughout human history from the wheel invented in ancient times to the personal computer of the late twentieth century.

People have always needed transport to travel and carry goods. For much of history, they used wheeled carts, which relied on human or animal muscles to pull them. In the eighteenth century, the steam engine revolutionised transport – a machine carried the load instead. The steam engine led to the beginning of the railways, which could transport large amounts of goods and people faster than ever before. It also provided power for machinery, promoting the growth of factories during the Industrial Revolution.

Fifteenth century: Johannes Gutenberg demonstrates the first printed sheet from his printing press.

Nineteenth century: Thomas Edison working on the electric light in his laboratory.

Industry and the way we work could not have developed without a way of measuring the time. From the late seventeenth century, accurate clocks allowed traders and businesspeople to arrange meetings and deliveries. As industry grew from the late eighteenth century, employees learnt the discipline of fixed shifts.

The light bulb, invented in the nineteenth century, brought artificial light to factories, businesses and homes so that activities could continue day and night.

Twentieth century: a family watching
their new television set (1948).

Other key inventions involved communications. Until the Middle Ages, few people
knew what was happening outside their town or village. The fifteenth-century
invention of the printing press led to the mass production of books, magazines
and newspapers, and ideas spread rapidly. Further inventions allowed people to
communicate with others across the world. From the nineteenth century, they could
send a telegram and talk on the telephone. The twentieth century saw television
beaming programmes directly into living rooms. While computers gave people
a window to the world from their home, letting them connect with individuals,
businesses and organisations. The internet has further broadened this knowledge.

Medical inventions have saved many lives: the introduction of anaesthetics in the
mid-nineteenth century permitted surgeons to carry out operations without causing
horrific pain to the patient. Other discoveries have made it easier to attack and
kill: gunpowder (which was probably invented in China) was used in guns from the
thirteenth century, and warfare grew increasingly deadly.

Ten further inventions that have transformed our world are included on
pages 26–7, and you can probably think of many more yourself!

THE WHEEL

Can you imagine life before the invention of the wheel? People had to lug heavy goods round on their backs or load them on to animals, and walk everywhere. Luckily, some had the bright idea of placing a load over a tree trunk and rolling it along. They also used sledges to pull things along the ground. Next, they placed the sledge on the tree-trunk roller – much easier! Over time, the roller developed grooves in it from the weight. People realised a lighter roller was easier to move, so they made the middle part of the roller thinner. Eventually, the thin middle part turned into a separate axle, fixed at each end to the wheels.

Mesopotamian wheel, about 3500 BCE.

Pictures from Sumeria and Mesopotamia (modern Iraq) show that the wheel had been created by 3500 BCE. It gradually adapted and improved over the centuries.

Around 2000 BCE, chariots with spoked wheels, which made the wheel structure lighter, appeared in ancient Egypt. The wheel had a hub (middle part), spokes and a rim (outer part). The wheel we recognise today had arrived.

To drive any car, the steering wheel is essential for changing its direction.

The war chariot of Egyptian king Ramses II, thirteenth century BCE.

CA. 3500 BCE: FIRST WHEELS APPEAR IN ASIA AND EUROPE ... 1700S: EUROPEANS BRING

SOME OTHER USES OF WHEELS

• Pulleys use wheels linked by rope to lift heavy things.

• Steering wheels are used to steer cars.

• Potter's wheels are for making pottery.

Changing the world

The Romans (c.500 BCE–400 CE) used a variety of wheeled vehicles. They rode in chariots for fighting and hunting, and raced in them for sport. Farmers used two-wheeled carts, and traders transported goods in heavy, four-wheeled wagons. There were passenger coaches, too. The use of the wheel spread throughout Europe and Asia. Europeans brought the wheel to the Americas in the sixteenth century and to sub-Saharan Africa in the nineteenth century. The basic design changed little until the late nineteenth century, when rubber tyres inflated with air were created to protect the wheel and reduce the shock from bumpy roads. Wheels have found their way into all forms of modern transport, from the humble bicycle to trains, cars and the landing gear of aircraft.

WHEEL TO THE AMERICAS ... 1800S: WHEEL SPREADS TO SUB-SAHARAN AFRICA ...

7

THE CLOCK

For many hundreds of years, people puzzled over how to measure time accurately. Ancient peoples measured time by looking at the sun's position using sundials. As the sun fell on an object, it created a shadow and the length of that shadow changed during the day. They knew that when the sun was right above them, it was midday. It was not much good on a cloudy day though! Around 1500 BCE, ancient Egyptians invented water clocks, using the steady dripping of water to measure time – but after a few hours the water ran out. From 700 to 1000 CE, Arab scientists improved the sundial – yet it still relied on the sun. What else could be used to tell the time?

Accurate timekeeping is essential for sports events nowadays.

Digital clocks

Modern digital clocks have an electric power supply to run them. An electronic timebase 'ticks' accurately while a counter changes the hours, minutes and seconds. The time is often displayed on a Liquid Crystal Display (LCD) screen.

An eighteenth-century-style bronze clock.

The first mechanical clocks in the fourteenth century were driven by weights but were inaccurate. In 1583, scientist Galileo had a brainwave. He noticed that a pendulum always takes the same amount of time to swing back and forth. It was perfect to use in a clock! In 1656, Dutch scientist Christiaan Huygens used Galileo's clever idea to make a pendulum clock. By the late seventeenth century, clocks could measure time right down to the second.

CA 1500 BCE: WATER CLOCK INVENTED ... 1656: FIRST PENDULUM CLOCK MADE ...

> 66 I remember that the idea occurred to him that the pendulum could be adapted to clocks with weights or springs ... he hoping that the very even and natural motions of the pendulum would correct all the defects [faults] in the art of clocks. 99
>
> VINCENZO VIVIANI,
> ASSISTANT TO GALILEO, 1641

Changing the world

Accurate timekeeping was essential for the development of trade and business. Traders and businesspeople could arrange meetings or exchange goods, and workers knew when they needed to arrive for a job. However, pendulum clocks were useless at sea – the metal or wood materials expanded or contracted depending on the temperature, changing the length of the pendulum swing. In 1735, Englishman John Harrison invented a chronometer, a clock that was accurate enough to be used on voyages. This improved navigation and allowed European explorers to travel all around the world. In the early twentieth century, electrical clocks were invented, which did not need winding up like mechanical ones. Clocks for the home became cheap and popular, and no one had an excuse for being late for appointments!

GUNPOWDER

Chinese inventors in the ninth century were convinced they could concoct a special formula to lengthen life. But, one day, their latest mixture of chemicals exploded in their faces. Quite by accident, they had discovered gunpowder – the world's first explosive.

In contrast to extending life, the Chinese realised that this invention had deadly possibilities as a weapon. In the thirteenth century, soldiers attached small packages of gunpowder to their arrows and lit them to hurl fiery missiles at their Mongol enemies. They also launched gunpowder bombs with catapults.

British soldiers firing a cannon in the First World War.

Around the same time, the Arabs discovered gunpowder and used it to build the first gun, a bamboo tube that used gunpowder to fire an arrow. Across the trade routes between Europe and the Middle East, the lethal invention spread rapidly. By 1350, gunpowder was used in cannon: the force of the explosion fired out a stone or metal ball, which hurtled at high speed towards the enemy. England and France battled each other with cannon in the Hundred Years' War (1337–1453), and the Ottoman Turks used them to conquer Constantinople in 1453.

By the mid-fifteenth century, handguns for individual soldiers appeared – they were simply mini cannon. Over the following centuries, gun design improved rapidly. Guns became more accurate, lighter and easier to use.

In ancient China, gunpowder was sometimes used as fireworks by emperors to entertain their guests.

800S: CHINESE INVENT GUNPOWDER ... BY 1350: GUNPOWDER IS USED IN CANNON ...

> **Some have heated together sulphur, realgar and saltpeter with honey; smoke and flames result, so that their hands and faces have been burnt, and even the whole house where they were working burned down.**
>
> **FIRST REFERENCE TO GUNPOWDER FROM A CHINESE TEXT, AROUND MID-NINTH CENTURY**

Changing the world

Some people used guns to hunt animals for food, and by 1700 gunpowder was used in mining operations in Germany. Yet, the greatest impact was on warfare. The Europeans who sailed overseas from the fifteenth century to explore other lands were heavily armed. They had more powerful weapons than the people they encountered in the Americas, and later in Asia and Africa. With superior military forces, the European explorers defeated the native inhabitants and seized their lands.

... 1400S: EUROPEANS USE GUNS TO CONQUER THE AMERICAS ...

THE PRINTING PRESS

Until the mid-fifteenth century in Europe, if you wanted to write a book, you wrote it by hand. To make copies, you had to write it out again – an extremely slow and boring job. Generally, only Church people had books, which were all about religion and written in Latin. Most people had never seen a book and they could not read.

In the eighth century, the Chinese had worked out how to print characters (symbols that stood for ideas or words) by applying ink to wooden blocks and putting paper over the top – just as you can use decorative rubber stamps today. However, it still took ages to print pages of text.

PREPARING PAGES

In Gutenberg's time, a skilled worker could assemble 2,000 characters or letters in an hour, ready for printing. That was super-fast at the time. Today, a computer can do the same job in just 2 seconds!

A modern printing press, based on Gutenberg's original design.

German inventor Johannes Gutenberg created a remarkable printing press in the mid-fifteenth century, one of the greatest innovations of all time. It could print entire pages with moveable type, quickly and efficiently. Gutenberg arranged the metal blocks with raised letters – the type – into words, and arranged the words to form sentences. He arranged the sentences of a page on a tray, put ink on the type and laid paper on top. With a machine, he pressed the paper against the type to print the page. Gutenberg printed the page as many times as he wanted. Then he changed the letters and reused them for another page.

Gutenberg examines the first page printed with his printing press.

Changing the world

Gutenberg's printing press made printing faster, easier and cheaper. His invention spread like wildfire throughout Europe. Now, large numbers of books were published and the first newspapers appeared. Many more people learnt to read and write, and they demanded books in their own languages about all kinds of subjects. A surge of interest arose in the ideas of ancient Greece and Rome, and books about science, government, art and philosophy spread widely. This was the age of the Renaissance, a flowering of learning that could not have developed without Gutenberg's extraordinary printing press.

INVENTS THE PRINTING PRESS ... 1600S: NEWSPAPERS APPEAR IN EUROPE AND JAPAN ...

13

THE STEAM ENGINE

In 1829, crowds gathered in Rainhill, northern England for the competition to demonstrate the best and fastest locomotive. The winner would receive a prize and their steam-engine design would be used to build trains for the world's first railway. George Stephenson's *Rocket* travelled faster than the others, climbed a hill and did not break down. It was the clear winner!

Before the steam engine, goods were carried by road or water. When the Industrial Revolution began in the eighteenth century, canals were built across Britain, and horse-drawn barges transported heavy goods, such as coal and pottery, at walking pace. Industry relied on wind and water power. Windmills used wind power to turn stones to grind grain, but only worked when it was breezy. Water mills used water flowing through rivers for the same purpose, but had to be located by water.

Excited crowds at the Rainhill locomotive trials of 1829.

In 1705, English inventor Thomas Newcomen produced the steam engine, which used steam power to pump water out of mines. Scottish inventor James Watt improved on it in 1765; his steam engine provided more power with less fuel. Steam engines were used to power the new factories. They proved perfect for transport, too. In 1814, George Stephenson built his first locomotive (a steam engine on wheels) that ran on rails and could pull several wagons. In 1825, he was the first to use a locomotive to pull a passenger train and was hired to build the first railway, between Liverpool and Manchester.

> 66 To show that it [the *Rocket*] had been working quite within its powers, Mr Stephenson ordered it to be ... detached from all incumbrance [without carriages], and in making two trips it moved at the astonishing rate of 35 miles [56 kilometres] an hour. 99
>
> **REPORT TO THE DIRECTORS OF THE LIVERPOOL AND MANCHESTER RAILWAY, 1831**

James Watt's first steam engine, *Fairbottom*, built in 1760.

Changing the world

Steam power soon replaced less reliable wind and water power. The steam engine allowed the massive growth of factories and of coal and iron mining. Stephenson's locomotive led to the development of railways across Britain. By 1850, Britain's railways and factories made it the wealthiest country in the world, and steam engines spread throughout Europe and North America.

STEAM ENGINE ... 1825: STEPHENSON USES A LOCOMOTIVE TO PULL A TRAIN ...

15

ANAESTHETICS

In 1846, dentist William Morton announced he would publicly demonstrate the use of an anaesthetic for the first time in the operating theatre. His colleague, Dr Warren, prepared the terrified patient in front of an excited audience of medical students and surgeons. Operations were usually noisy affairs, with the patient screaming in agony. But after using Morton's ether inhaler, the patient passed out and lay unconscious as his tumour (lump) was removed. The operation was pain-free and silent.

Before anaesthetics, surgery was used as a last resort to save lives. Surgeons could carry out amputations (cutting off a limb), but they could not cut into the abdomen, chest or skull because it would take too long and prove unbearably painful. Patients had to be strapped to the operating table so they could not escape. They often died from shock, loss of blood or infection.

HOW ANAESTHETICS WORK

If you have an anaesthetic, for example, at the dentist, the drug stops the passage of pain signals along the nerves from your mouth to your brain. So your brain does not detect the pain.

Anaesthetics allow complicated surgery such as this hand transplant to take place.

William Morton gives a patient ether for the first time.

There had been many attempts to reduce the pain of surgery. They included bashing the patient on the head to knock them out, giving them alcohol or a drug called opium, or applying ice to numb a body part. In the early nineteenth century, nitrous oxide, known as 'laughing gas' was given. But none of these methods worked as well as ether.

EARLY 1800S: LAUGHING GAS USED TO DULL PAIN ... 1846 WILLIAM MORTON USES

Changing the world

Anaesthetics provided a way of stopping the pain patients experienced during surgery. Surgeons could take their time and were able to operate on all areas of the body for the first time. The early anaesthetics were inhaled and often had nasty side-effects. In the early twentieth century, safer types were introduced that were injected and sent the patient off to sleep quickly and pleasantly. For minor operations, local anaesthetics could be used to numb the part of the body being operated on, while the patient stayed awake. From the 1930s, doctors were specially trained to become anaesthetists. Nowadays, they are involved in childbirth, emergency care and pain management. Their role is key to safe operations.

ETHER AS ANAESTHETIC ... 1930S: DOCTORS CAN TRAIN AS ANAESTHETISTS ...

THE TELEPHONE

In 1876, inventor Alexander Graham Bell spoke the first words ever spoken by telephone to his assistant: 'Mr Watson – come here – I want to see you.' Thomas Watson heard his words and obeyed the call.

Bell was not the only person trying to invent the telephone. But he registered his discovery first and went down in history as the creator of this world-changing invention.

When Bell and Watson demonstrated the device that year at the Centennial Exposition in Philadelphia, the United States of America (USA), the public were delighted. The following year, Bell set up the Bell Telephone Company, starting a communications revolution. Cheap and simple to use, the telephone remains the most popular form of communication in the world.

Delivering a telegram in the USA.

Before the telephone, the main way to contact others across a distance was by posting a letter. From the early nineteenth century, inventors experimented with ways of sending messages using electricity. In 1832, Samuel F. B. Morse designed the telegraph. Messages called telegrams were sent over wires using a code with dots and dashes, named Morse Code after its inventor. By 1900, telegraph wires crossed the world and messages could be sent instantly over huge distances.

1876: ALEXANDER GRAHAM BELL INVENTS TELEPHONE ... 1915: PHONE CALLS CAN BE MADE

> 66 Great discoveries and improvements invariably involve the cooperation of many minds. I may be given credit for having blazed the trail, but when I look at the subsequent developments I feel the credit is due to others rather than to myself. 99
>
> ALEXANDER GRAHAM BELL

Alexander Graham Bell makes the first long-distance call from New York to Chicago, 1892.

Changing the world

By 1915, people could make phone calls across the USA. Telephone systems spread throughout the industrialised countries, speeding up communication. In 1927, it became possible to make calls between Europe and the USA. From the 1970s, fax machines used telephone wires to allow people to send text and pictures. Later that decade, mobile telephones appeared. Instead of being linked by wires like traditional phones, they are connected by radio waves that travel through the air. At the start of the twenty-first century, people could use smartphones to communicate by voice, text and email while on the move, as well as send photos and videos, play games and use the internet.

THE LIGHT BULB

Until the nineteenth century, most people around the world lit their homes with candles. A lit candle did not last long, the light was poor and it could easily cause a fire. In the early nineteenth century, gas lighting became popular in British and American homes and for street lamps. However, gas lighting was not perfect as gas was dangerous and there was a risk of fire. A better lighting solution was needed.

Once electric power had been developed, the race was on to find ways of using it for lighting. American inventor Sir Joseph Wilson Swan was determined to win the contest. In 1860, he created the world's first electric light bulb. However, the first bulb did not last long and the light was feeble. Thomas Edison was the other main contender. Known as the 'wizard' for his many inventions, he was also working furiously to produce a light bulb.

In 1878, Swan proudly presented the first incandescent lamp. He enclosed a filament (thread) to pass the electricity through in a glass bulb, pumped out the air to create a vacuum and sealed the glass. One year later, Edison produced a light bulb that was similar. But he also created power lines and all the equipment needed to build a complete lighting system. With this impressive collection of inventions, Edison was celebrated as the creator of the light bulb.

HOW INCANDESCENT LIGHT BULBS WORK

A filament in the bulb is heated by passing an electric current through it so it glows. The filament is in a vacuum so it does not burn itself out in air.

Thomas Edison in the laboratory working on his electric light.

1878: SIR JOSEPH WILSON SWAN MAKES FIRST LIGHT BULB ... 1879: THOMAS EDISON

Changing the world

By 1900, electric lighting lit homes, factories and businesses all over the industrialised world. Factories could operate all night, boosting productivity. No longer did people have to strain their eyes to work, study or play in poor candle light during dark evenings. Outdoors, street lighting made it safer to walk around at night. During the 1930s, fluorescent lamps were developed – long tubes producing bright white light that used only about a third of the energy of incandescent lights and lasted longer. They were quickly adopted for workplaces, such as factories and offices. In the late twentieth century, as people tried to reduce their energy use, energy-efficient light bulbs appeared, such as compact fluorescent lights and LED lamps for home light fittings.

THE TELEVISION

In 1953, a young British princess, Princess Elizabeth, was to be crowned queen. People were hugely excited about this historic event, yet few could travel to London for the big day. Fortunately, the number of television (TV) owners was growing rapidly. On Coronation Day on 2 June 1953, more than half of the adult population in Britain (and many children) crowded into neighbours' homes, churches and hospitals to watch the queen being crowned on television – the highest viewing figure at the time and a milestone for TV broadcasting.

Once the telephone appeared, scientists then dreamt of being able to transmit images alongside sound. Several countries claimed that one of their scientists invented television, including John Logie Baird in Britain, Kenjiro Takayanagi in Japan and Karl Braun in Germany. In fact, a series of inventions enabled the changing of light into electric signals. Televisions were first demonstrated in the USA and Britain in the 1920s, and the British Broadcasting Company (BBC) started programming in 1936. American television companies began broadcasting in 1941. Early television sets had black-and-white pictures and from the 1950s colour televisions appeared.

New Yorkers watch the coronation of Queen Elizabeth II on a display TV.

In the 1940s, it was still very unusual for a family to own a TV.

The percentage of American homes with a TV grew astonishingly quickly:

Year	Percentage
1950	9%
1955	65%
1960	87%
1980	98%
2009	99%

Changing the world

Television became one of the most popular forms of communication, enabling people to access news, information and entertainment programmes from the comfort of their own homes. It caught on particularly quickly in the USA; by 1962, 90 per cent of households had a television set, and they watched for an average of five hours a day! Much of the world soon adopted the TV-watching habit. From the 1970s, cable TV launched, using signals travelling along underground cables. Satellite TV started up, too, with a signal beamed from a satellite above the earth to people's satellite dishes. Cable and satellite television companies provided a huge range of networks, from sports and music to the weather. From the 1990s, networks switched to digital systems, converting their signals into computer code. Digital television provided clearer pictures and sound. Television programming companies sold their products worldwide, so people around the globe could watch the same shows and access them on different devices, including DVDs, computers and mobile phones.

THE PERSONAL COMPUTER (PC)

In 1974, American designer Ed Roberts created the first personal computer (PC), the Altair 8800. He thought he would only sell a few hundred to electronics fans because people had to assemble it themselves, and all it did was play a game with flashing lights. When thousands sold in the first month, he was amazed.

Computers had existed since the Second World War (1939–1945) but they were expensive, bulky machines and only experts could use them. One of the first was ENIAC. It weighed 30.5 tonnes (30 tons) and measured 5.5 x 24 metres (18 x 80 feet) – almost the size of a tennis court! In 1971, American engineer Marcian E. Hoff put the basic elements of a computer on a silicon chip called a microprocessor. The development of microprocessors in the 1970s made it possible to make much smaller computers.

Apple unveils its 1984 computer to compete with PCs.

In 1976, Steven Jobs and Stephen Wozniak formed Apple Computer and the following year brought out the Apple II, with high-quality colour graphics. Early computers like this could only play simple games and do calculations, but were expensive. This changed after IBM introduced the Personal Computer in 1981, and competitors brought out similar machines. The price of computers fell dramatically so that businesses could afford them. Companies such as Microsoft, set up in 1975 by Bill Gates and Paul Allen, produced programs for PCs so people could create text and graphics and do their accounts. This gave businesses a reason to buy computers.

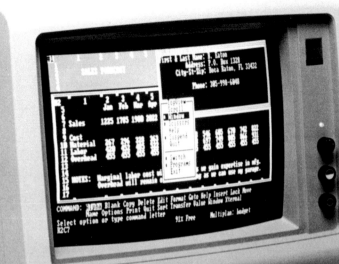

> 66 Over 20 years ago, even before I helped to co-found Microsoft, I saw a connected future ... I called that future the wired world. 99
>
> **PAUL ALLEN,**
> **CO-FOUNDER OF MICROSOFT, 1998**

An IBM computer from 1984 – PCs became cheaper and more popular than Apple computers.

Changing the world

By the 1990s, PCs had become much cheaper, yet were fast and powerful enough to run extremely complex programs. Multimedia CD-Roms appeared, enabling PC users to access pictures, videos and music from a CD. These were soon overtaken by the internet.

Now, practically every business uses PCs for work and communications, and many people in developed countries have one at home. PCs have changed the way people access information and how they connect with their friends, family and work colleagues.

10 OTHER IDEAS THAT CHANGED THE WORLD

1. The boat

As long as 10,000 years ago, people worked out how to make simple rafts from logs tied together and canoes carved out of logs. They used them for fishing and travel. Around 4500 BCE, the Egyptians developed sailing ships, which permitted people to travel long distances across the water to trade.

2. The plough

A plough turns and breaks up the soil, ready for growing crops. The Romans used light ploughs, without wheels. They had a blade and were pulled by oxen (bulls). In medieval northern Europe, the heavy-wheeled plough was developed to turn the heavy soil there. The plough was adopted across the world, greatly speeding up farmers' work.

3. Sanitation

Toilets are vital for public health and hygiene; without sewage pipes to safely remove waste from homes, diseases spread easily. Either the Scots or the ancient Greeks first built toilets. Flushable toilets were invented at the end of the eighteenth century and spread around the world, vastly improving hygiene.

4. Paper

The Chinese invented paper about 2,000 years ago, using linen fibres. The method gradually spread around the world. From the nineteenth century, people started to use machines to make paper from wood pulp (softened wood), making it cheaper and quicker to produce supplies for books, newspapers and packaging.

5. The compass

The first compasses were made in twelfth-century China and Europe, after people found that when a magnetised piece of iron floated in water, it pointed north. Later compasses were mounted under a card and placed in a box. The magnetic compass helped sailors to navigate at sea. leading to a huge expansion in trade and exploration.

6. The radio

In 1901, Italian scientist Guglielmo Marconi succeeded in sending the first radio signals from England to Canada. In 1920, the first radio stations were set up in the USA. In the early twentieth century, radio became the first electronic mass medium. Providing news and entertainment, it proved enormously popular and remained the most widely available form of media despite the introduction of television.

7. Refrigeration

Until the twentieth century, few people were able to keep their food cool and safe to eat. In the mid-nineteenth century, various refrigeration (cooling) systems were invented for industry, and people bought ice to use at home. In the 1930s, after the development of small electric motors, refrigerators were made for homes. The invention spread across the world, allowing safe food storage.

8. The internal-combustion engine

The first successful internal-combustion engine was invented by German engineer Nikolaus Otto in 1876. It burnt fuel petrol inside the engine, and was lighter and more powerful than a steam engine. The internal-combustion engine made it possible to develop cars, one of the main forms of transport today.

9. Penicillin

In 1928, Alexander Fleming made one of the greatest discoveries of the twentienth century. He found out that a kind of mould stopped bacteria from growing. Knowing that bacteria caused many diseases, Fleming developed the antibiotic penicillin from the mould. By the 1930s, it was used to treat infections caused by bacteria. Penicillin has saved millions of lives.

10. Space exploration

Both the Soviet Union and the USA developed the technology to launch and fly spacecraft. In 1957, the Soviet Union began the space age by launching the first satellite into space, Sputnik I. In 1969. American astronaut Neil Armstrong was the first person to walk on the moon. Since then, thousands of missions have gone into space for communications, navigation and scientific research into our solar system. In 2014, the Rosetta mission's lander became the first spacecraft to land on a comet.

TIMELINE

Around 3000 BCE
Great civilisations arise in Babylonia and Assyria in south-west Asia and in ancient Egypt.

Around 2000 BCE
The final stage of building Stonehenge, a place of worship in England, takes place.

Around 30 CE
Christianity is born.

476
The fall of the last Roman Emperor, Romulus Augustulus, leads to the decline of the Roman Empire.

1789
The French Revolution breaks out and sets up a republic to govern the country.

1776
The United States of America declares independence from Britain and sets up its own government.

Eighteenth and nineteenth centuries
The Industrial Revolution takes place in Europe and the USA, bringing huge advances in the development of machinery for factories, farming and transport.

1850s
Louis Pasteur develops pasteurisation, a way of preserving food by heating it to kill the germs.

1865
The American Civil War (1861–65) between the northern and southern states ends with the victory of the north.

2001
Members of a terrorist group called Al-Qaeda hijack four aeroplanes in the USA and fly two of them into the World Trade Center in New York; about 3,000 are killed in total.

1989
The East German government is forced out of power, the borders are opened with West Germany, and the Berlin Wall is torn down.

1969
The USA lands a spacecraft on the moon: Neil Armstrong and Buzz Aldrin are the first men to walk on the moon.

7th century
The Islamic faith is established.

1095
The Crusades begin – military campaigns by European Christians to control the holy places of the Middle East.

1215
In England, the Magna Carta is signed, an agreement that states that the king of England has to follow the law and gives rights to the English people.

1348–50
The Black Death kills up to half of the population of Europe.

Sixteenth and seventeenth centuries
The Scientific Revolution in Europe leads to many advances in astronomy, biology and physics and improvements in navigation.

1492
The explorer Christopher Columbus arrives in the Americas and claims several Caribbean islands for Spain.

1903
Wilbur and Orville Wright build the first aeroplane.

1914
The First World War breaks out after the assassination of Archduke Franz Ferdinand.

1917
The Russian Revolution takes place in Russia, ending the rule of the Tsars and leading to a Communist government.

1949
Communist leader Mao Zedong takes control of China and forms the People's Republic of China.

1947
India gains independence from British rule; over the following thirty years, most Asian and African countries also become independent.

1945
The USA drops nuclear bombs on Hiroshima and Nagasaki, killing tens of thousands of people instantly and leading to the end of the Second World War.

1939
The Second World War begins when Germany invades Poland, and Britain and France declare war on Germany.

GLOSSARY

abdomen The part of the body that contains the stomach and the bowels.

anaesthetic A drug that stops a person from feeling pain in the whole body or part of the body.

assassinate To murder an important person, especially for political reasons.

axle A long, straight piece of wood or metal that connects a pair of wheels on a vehicle.

bacteria The smallest and simplest forms of life, which often cause disease.

broadcasting Making and sending out radio and television programmes.

cable A set of wires, covered in plastic or rubber, that carries electricity or telephone signals.

cannon Used in the past, a large, heavy gun, usually on wheels, that fires solid metal or stone balls.

chariot An open vehicle with two wheels, pulled by horses, used in ancient times in battle and for racing.

Communist Describing the theory of a social and political system where there is common ownership of production and the running of services. In practice, in the Soviet Union between 1922 to 1991, however, this meant a single, authoritarian government was in control.

compact fluorescent light An energy-saving lamp designed to replace the older incandescent lamp.

conquer To overcome and take control.

convert To change the form, character or function of something.

digital Using a system of receiving and sending information as a series of ones and zeros – this is how computers work.

electric current A flow of electric charge.

electronic Having many small parts that control and direct a small electric current. The study of electric currents is called electronics.

energy efficient Using as little energy as possible to do a job.

ether A clear liquid made from alcohol that was used in the past as a medicine to put people to sleep before an operation.

fluorescent Producing bright light.

graphics Designs, drawings or pictures.

gunpowder Explosive powder used in bombs or fireworks.

incandescent lamp One of the main forms of electric light that was made and sold from the late nineteenth century onwards.

Industrial Revolution The period in the eighteenth and nineteenth centuries in Europe and the USA, when machines began to be used to do work, and industry grew rapidly.

inhaler A portable device for administering a drug which is to be breathed in.

LED lamp A light bulb that uses up to 85 per cent less energy than an incandescent light bulb.

locomotive A railway engine that pulls a train.

magnetised When a metal is made to behave like a magnet.

mass medium Different forms of media technologies that are intended to reach a large audience by mass communication.

microprocessor A small unit of a computer that controls all the other parts.

Middle Ages The period of European history between ancient and modern times. The Middle Ages began with the Fall of Rome in the fifth century and ended with the Renaissance.

missile An object which is forcibly propelled at a target.

Mongol In the thirteenth century, a people who had an empire in Central Asia and came into conflict with China.

navigation Planning a route for a ship or other vehicle to a particular place and taking it there.

pendulum A long, straight part in a clock, with a weight at the end that moves regularly from side to side to keep the time.

Renaissance The revival of European art and literature under the influence of classical models in the fourteenth to sixteenth centuries.

Republic Describing the political system where power is held by the people and their elected representatives.

satellite An electronic device that is sent into space and moves around the Earth (or another planet). It is used for communicating by radio and television and for providing information.

Science Revolution When developments in mathematics, physics, astronomy, biology and chemistry transformed views of society and nature.

telegraph A method of sending messages called telegrams over long distances, using wires carrying electrical signals.

transmit To send an electronic signal, radio or television broadcast.

unconscious When a person is in a sleep-like state because of illness or having been given an anaesthetic, and is not able to use their senses.

vacuum A space that is completely empty of all substances, including air.

warfare The activities involved in war or conflict.

FURTHER INFORMATION

Books

The Greatest Inventions of All Time,
Jillian Powell, Wayland (2015)

The World in Infographics – Technology, Jon
Richards and Ed Simkins, Wayland (2014)

Who's Who in Science and Technology,
Bob Fowke, Wayland (2014)

*Barmy Biogs – Bonkers Boffins, Inventors
and Other Eccentric Eggheads*, Paul Mason,
Wayland (2013)

Websites

For students:
A History of the World in 100 Objects,
by Neil MacGregor
www.britishmuseum.org/explore/a_history_of_
the_world.aspx

Ten objects from the Science Museum's
collection that changed the world
www.sciencemuseum.org.uk/Centenary.aspx

For teachers:
Inventions That Changed Our World
http://teacher.scholastic.com/lessonrepro/
lessonplans/theme/inventions.htm

Podcasts

A History of the World in 100 Objects
www.bbc.co.uk/podcasts/series/ahow/all

DVD

Wallace and Gromit's World of Invention
(2entertain, 2010)

INDEX

DISCOVER MORE ABOUT WHO AND WHAT HAS CHANGED THE COURSE OF HUMAN HISTORY!

10 ARTWORKS THAT CHANGED THE WORLD
9780750291361

10 EVENTS THAT CHANGED THE WORLD
9780750291279

10 IDEAS THAT CHANGED THE WORLD
9780750291392

10 PEOPLE THAT CHANGED THE WORLD
9780750291293

WAYLAND
www.waylandbooks.co.uk